Guitar Metho

Book with Audio Access

by
Peter Vogl

The Follow-up to Guitar Method 1
For Acoustic or Electric Guitar

For online Audio Access to all of the audio tracks in this course,
go to this address on the web:

http://cvls.com/extras/gm2/

INTRODUCTION

Guitar Method 2 is the follow-up course to *Guitar Method 1*. This clear step-by-step method represents the first major innovation in note reading books in the last 50 years and draws upon the extensive teaching experience of one of the world's leading guitar instructors. The method teaches you practical songs, scales, and chords that are currently used today, which will enable you to apply what you have learned to the songs that you want to play. The Audio Tracks that come with this method are recorded by top studio musicians and will enable you to hear every exercise and example in this course. In addition, there are 57 play along jam tracks that will let you play along with a full band, which not only is fun but will help you perfect your timing and ability to play with others. These tracks will also let you practice and perform for student recitals.

THE AUTHOR

Peter Vogl, the author of this book, has been a professional performer and teacher in the Atlanta area for over twenty years. He was raised in Michigan and went to college at the University of Georgia, where he majored in classical guitar performance. He also did post graduate work at James Madison University. Peter has set up and directed six different schools of music in the Atlanta area and currently works at Jan Smith Studios as a session player and guitar instructor. He has written several instructional courses including *Introduction to Blues Guitar Book & DVD, Rock Guitar Book & DVD, The Guitarist's Tablature Book, The Guitarist's Chord Book, The Guitarist's Scale Book, The Guitarist's Music Theory Book, Electric Licks & Solos, Country Licks & Solos,* and the *Let's Jam! CD Series* (eight different jam along CDs).

WATCH & LEARN PRODUCTS REALLY WORK

For over 30 years, Watch & Learn has revolutionized music instructional courses by developing well thought out, step by step instructional methods that were tested for effectiveness on beginners before publication. Each course is developed by top instructors that actively teach and are in touch with the current needs of students. Coupled with the consistent high standards of Watch & Learn, this has dramatically improved the success and enjoyment of beginning musicians and has set the standard for music instruction today. This easy to understand course will help you tremendously on your journey to having fun and becoming a well rounded guitarist.

AUDIO TRACKS ACCESS

There are two sets of audio tracks with this book. *Disc 1 - Exercises* contains all of the exercises in the book. The audio is mixed with the metronome on the right channel and the guitar on the left channel so you can isolate the metronome if you like. *Disc 2 - Songs* contains all of the songs performed with a live band. There are two versions of most songs, one with guitar playing along with the band and a second version with only the band so you can play along

This course includes online access to all of the audio tracks for the material in this book. Go to this address on the web:

http://cvls.com/extras/gm2/

COMPANION PRODUCTS

If the material in this book is too difficult for you, go to *Guitar Method 1* for a review and to build up your skill.

The Guitar Method 1 Book by Peter Vogl is a beginner guitar course designed for any guitarist who wants to learn how to read traditional music notation. You will learn how to read the notes on the staff as you play fun musical examples in different genres. Each exercise features an audio track playing just the basic notes and a second track featuring accompaniment from a full band. These backing tracks can be used as a recital piece to perform for family and friends. You will learn how to read notes, key signatures, chords and more. This exciting beginner guitar method will teach you how to actually play guitar and read music.

http://a.co/ctCPcja

The Guitarist's Chord Book by Peter Vogl is a 144 page book that contains over 900 chords with photos to clearly illustrate each chord and each note of the chord is labeled. Our ChordFinder System, using icons and letters, makes finding chords easy. It also contains a special moveable chords section with the most widely used shapes for each class of chord. Also contains Peter's Picks - goodies from Peter's bag of tricks to give you new sounds, shapes, and inspirations for song arrangements. The chord shapes have been reviewed by guitar teachers and players across the country. This is a must for guitar players of all levels.

http://a.co/0OLJ8GJ

The Guitarist's Scale Book by Peter Vogl is a complete scale encyclopedia for guitar with over 400 scales and modes. It contains scale diagrams with notation and tablature for each scale and tips on how and when to use each scale. Our ScaleFinder System, using icons and letters, makes scale finding easy. It also contains outside jazz scales, exotic scales, Peter's own Cross-Stringing scales, and easy to understand explanation of scales and modes. This is the only guitar scale book you'll ever need.

http://a.co/5vmp4Jd

The Guitarist's Music Theory Book by Peter Vogl is the first music theory book designed for guitar by a guitarist. The book explains music theory as it applies to the guitar and covers intervals, scales, chords, chord progressions, and the Nashville Number System. The included Audio CD features examples of all the music in the book and also an ear training section. The Music Theory Book was written to help all guitar players achieve a better understanding of the guitar and of the music they play.

http://a.co/0GMum16

You should also check out all of the instructional material on our websites, GuitarCompass.com and cvls.com.

TABLE OF CONTENTS

SECTION 1
GETTING STARTED

A REVIEW FROM GUITAR METHOD 1

For online Audio Access to all of the audio tracks in this course, go to this address on the web:

http://cvls.com/extras/gm2/

THE GUITAR

Your guitar should be stored in a neutral environment. This means not too cold, not too hot, not too wet, and not too dry. The wood in a guitar is subject to change and will expand or contract in response to its environment. Too much of any of these things could cause permanent damage. For example, never leave your guitar in your car for long periods of time during summer or winter months. Attics and basements tend to be poor locations for storing a guitar as well.

If you use a strap with your guitar to stand up and play, always keep a hand on the guitar. Straps won't always hold and a guitar falling from that height is never good. You can purchase strap locks to add another level of security, but if the strap itself breaks, the guitar may still fall.

The following photo shows the parts of a steel string guitar.

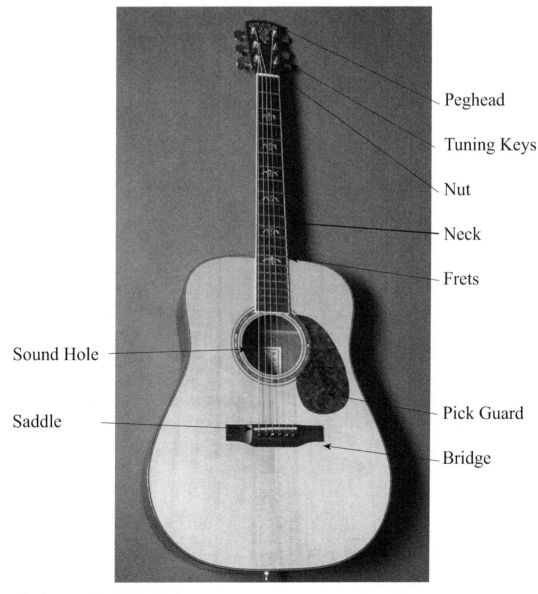

 TIP *Purchase a music stand. People who use one tend to practice up to 30% longer.*

1

TUNING THE GUITAR

Before playing the guitar, it must be tuned to standard pitch. If you have a piano at home, it can be used as a tuning source. The following picture shows which note on the piano to tune each open string of the guitar to.

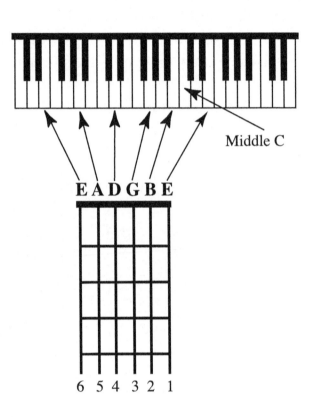

Note: If your piano hasn't been tuned recently, the guitar may not agree perfectly with a pitch pipe or tuning fork. Some older pianos are tuned a half step below standard pitch. In this case, use one of the following methods to tune.

AUDIO TRACKS

It is recommended that you tune your guitar to the Audio Tracks that accompanies this book so that you will be in tune when you play along with the songs and exercises.

ELECTRONIC TUNER

An electronic tuner is the fastest and most accurate way to tune a guitar. I highly recommend getting one. It may take months or years for a beginner to develop the skills to tune a guitar correctly by ear. Even then the electronic tuner is more precise and used by virtually every professional guitar player.

TIP *Never leave your instrument in a car or trunk during extreme heat or cold.*

RELATIVE TUNING

Relative tuning means to tune the guitar to itself and is used in the following situations:

1. When you do not have an electronic tuner or other source to tune from.
2. When you have only one note to tune from.

In the following example we will tune all of the strings to the 6th string of the guitar, which is an E note.

1. Place the ring finger of the left hand behind the 5th fret of the 6th string to fret the 1st note. Tune the 5th string open (not fretted) until it sounds like the 6th string fretted at the 5th fret.
2. Fret the 5th string at the 5th fret. Tune the 4th string open (not fretted) until it sounds like the 5th string at the 5th fret.
3. Fret the 4th string at the 5th fret. Tune the 3rd string open until it sounds like the 4th string at the 5th fret.
4. Fret the 3rd string at the 4th fret. Tune the 2nd string until it sounds like the 3rd string at the 4th fret.
5. Fret the 2nd string at the 5th fret. Tune the 1st string open until it sounds like the 2nd string at the 5th fret.

Now repeat the above procedure to fine tune the guitar. Until your ear develops, have your teacher or a guitar playing friend check the tuning to make sure it is correct.

The following diagram of the guitar fret board illustrates the above procedure.
Note - Old dull strings lose their tonal qualities and sometimes tune incorrectly.

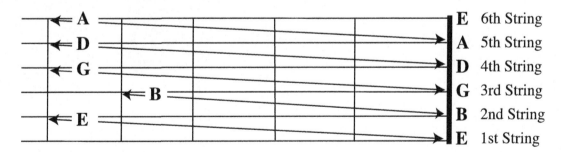

Check with your teacher or favorite music store to make sure your strings are in good playing condition.

Always keep an extra set of strings in your case. You never know when you will break one.

HOLDING THE GUITAR

CASUAL POSITION

There are two basic sitting positions for holding the guitar. The first and most common is the casual position. Sit erect with both feet on the floor and the guitar resting on your right thigh. The guitar should be braced against your chest with the right forearm so that the neck of the guitar doesn't move much when you change hand positions.

CLASSICAL POSITION

The second position is the classical position. Sit erect with your right foot on the floor and your left foot elevated on a footstool. The guitar rests on your left leg with the neck elevated. This position allows for a better back position and may make it easier for those who have back pain. It also allows for more freedom of movement of the left arm by raising the guitar neck and removing the left leg as an obstacle.

STANDING POSITION

When standing and using a strap, keep the guitar elevated for better technique, somewhere around waist high to chest high, depending on your build. Use a good strap or it may cause discomfort in the shoulders. A wide strap distributes the weight of the guitar better and is recommended.

TIP *Always use a case or gig bag when transporting your instrument from one place to another.*

THE PICK

SELECTING THE PICK

When you visit a music store, you will notice that there are almost as many pick styles and shapes as there are guitar players. A pick should feel comfortable in your hand and produce a clear, clean tone when picking or strumming the strings. This is the most popular pick shape.

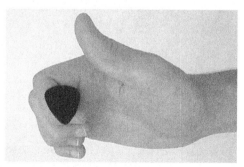

HOLDING THE PICK

The grip on a pick should provide control while feeling comfortable. The most common way of holding the pick is to curl the right index finger (Figure 1), place the pick in the first joint of the index finger with the point facing straight out (Figure 2), and then place the thumb firmly on the pick with the thumb parallel to the first joint (Figure 3).

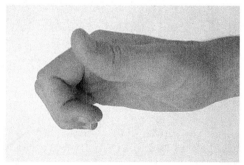

Figure 1

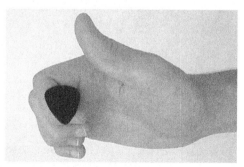

Figure 2

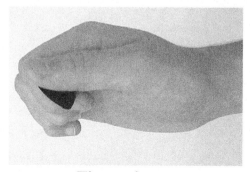

Figure 3

 TIP

Keep many extra picks around. They like to disappear, much like socks.

RIGHT HAND POSITION

Position the right hand so that the pick strikes the strings between the bridge and the fretboard. The top of the right forearm should be braced against the body of the guitar so that the right hand falls into a position towards the center of the sound hole. Do not rest your wrist or palm on the bridge. Too close to the bridge produces a bright tone and too far forward produces a tone that may be too dark. The right hand should be free with no part of the hand or wrist touching the guitar.

Bright   Correct   Too Dark   Wrist Not Resting on Guitar

LEFT HAND FINGERS

The index finger is the first finger, the middle finger is the second finger, the ring finger is the third finger and the pinky is the fourth finger. The thumb is not given a number since it is on the back of the neck.

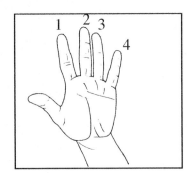

 *Use a guitar cloth to clean your guitar and wipe it down after you play.*

6

LEFT HAND POSITION

When positioning your left hand on the guitar, pay careful attention to several things. The left elbow should hang freely to the outside of the left leg. Don't let your elbow creep into a position resting on the left leg or more into the body. This will avoid undue stress on the elbow and wrist. The hand itself should be positioned so the fingers can stay in front of the guitar neck.

THUMB POSITION

The thumb placement can vary a little due to hand and body size. Our basic thumb position will be around half way up the back of the guitar neck. This is our *core position*, meaning use this position most of the time. There will be times when we use an elevated thumb position, but this may compromise technique. We will discuss when to do this at a later time. Smaller hands should have an even lower thumb placement. This allows for better stretching and finger dexterity.

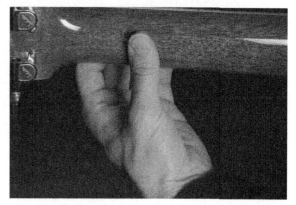

WRIST POSITION

The wrist should be below the guitar neck, which is our *wrist core position*.

TIP *A guitar should have a set-up every 6 months or so. Check with your local music store for this service.*

WHAT FRETS MEAN TO YOU

Frets are the little metal bars on the neck of the guitar. When pressing down on a string in a fret space, the sound of the note comes from the fret in front of the finger (or to the left in the photo below). This is very, very important. What this means is **when we are pressing down any string in any fret, we are not trying to hold the string against the wood of the guitar neck**. (Read above phrase again as reinforcement). We are holding the string down so it touches the fret in front of it.

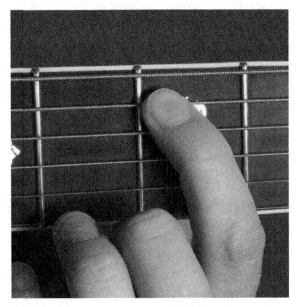
Finger at front of fret and good position

Finger in back of fret and poor position

CHORD DIAGRAMS

In this book you will find chord diagrams that will help you visualize where fingers should be placed on the guitar. Study the diagram below so that you will understand these diagrams when you see them.

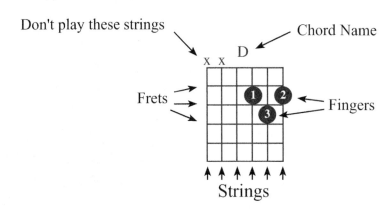

Once the frets on a guitar have large divots, they need to be replaced. This is called a fret job.

8

NOTE PARTS

Notes can have several different parts depending on what type of note they are.

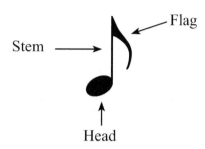

Flag

Stem ⟶

Head

NOTE RHYTHMS

The type of note tells us how many beats to hold it or what rhythm to play. A whole note, which is a hollow note head, typically lasts for four beats or counts. The half note, which has a hollow head and a stem, lasts for two beats. The quarter note, which has a solid head and a stem, lasts for one beat. The eighth note has a solid head, a stem and one flag and lasts for half of a beat. (Two eighth notes last the same amount of time as one quarter note). The sixteenth note has a solid head, stem, and two flags. It lasts for a quarter of a beat (Four sixteenth notes lasts the same amount of time as a quarter note).

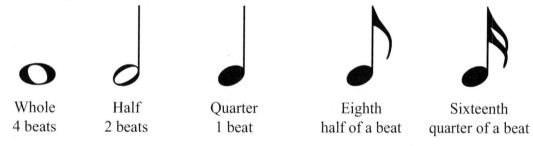

| Whole | Half | Quarter | Eighth | Sixteenth |
| 4 beats | 2 beats | 1 beat | half of a beat | quarter of a beat |

TIP *Using a guitar footstool may make practicing more comfortable and let you practice longer.*

The diagram below shows how many half, quarter, eighth, and sixteenth notes it would take to last the same amount of time as a whole note. Two half notes equal one whole note. Two quarter notes equal one half note. Two eighth notes equal one quarter note. Two sixteenth notes equal one eighth note.

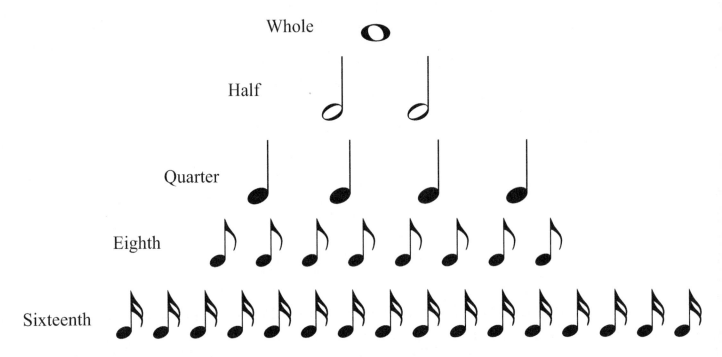

RESTS

When reading music, we also need to know when not to play. Rests tell us how much time to wait before we play again.

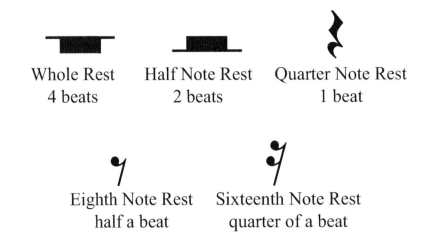

THE STAFF

The staff is where we place the notes telling us what pitch to play. The staff is made up of ledger lines and spaces.

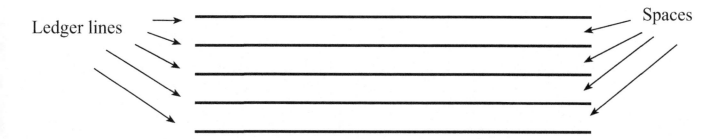

Ledger lines

Spaces

There are several elements added to the staff giving us more information. The clef sign tells us what pitches the lines and spaces represent. When playing guitar we use the treble clef.

Treble Clef

The treble clef sign tells us that the lines and spaces represent specific pitches. The spaces from the bottom up are the pitches F, A, C, E. The lines from the bottom up are E, G, B, D, F.

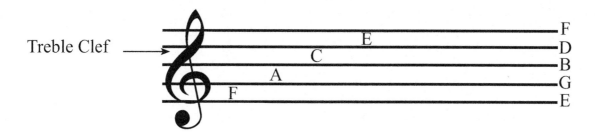

Treble Clef

BAR LINES

Bar lines are added to the staff to divide it into smaller units called measures or bars. This will make the staff easier to read and it will also tell us information about the rhythms and what notes are accented. Typically we accent the first beat in a measure. We will learn more about this as we learn about time signature.

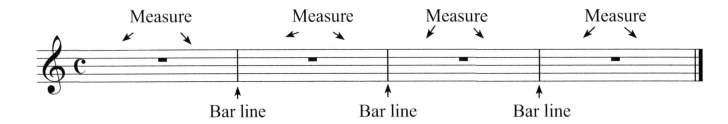

TIME SIGNATURE

Time signature is a symbol that tells us how many beats are in a measure. There are many time signatures and a few that are used more than others. Below are examples of the most frequently used time signatures.

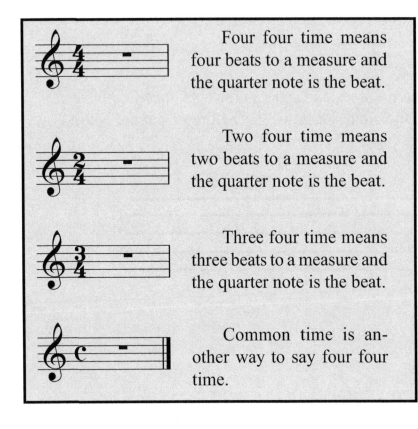

Four four time means four beats to a measure and the quarter note is the beat.

Two four time means two beats to a measure and the quarter note is the beat.

Three four time means three beats to a measure and the quarter note is the beat.

Common time is another way to say four four time.

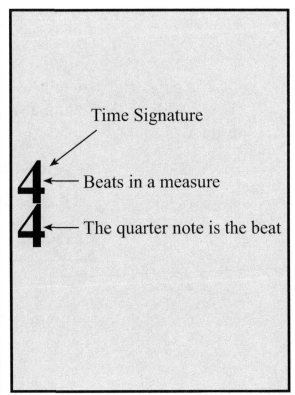

Time Signature

Beats in a measure

The quarter note is the beat

NOTES ON THE STAFF

Now we can see what the notes actually look like on the staff. Notes lower on the staff are lower in pitch. Notes higher on the staff are higher in pitch. Also notice the pick direction markings. These tell you what direction to play with your pick.

LEDGER LINES

We can go higher or lower than the five lines and spaces that make up the staff by adding extra ledger lines. It is like adding a line to the staff but we use just a small line. The reason we do this is to make the staff easier to read. Otherwise we would need a staff with many lines and spaces.

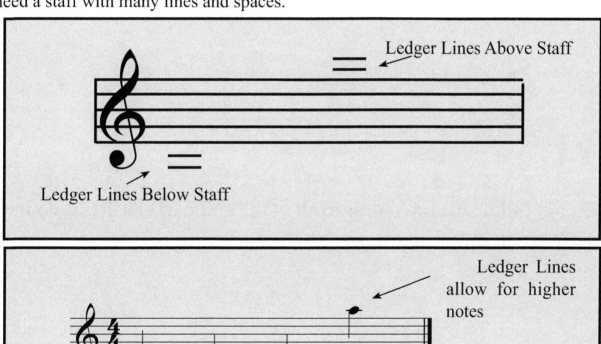

SECTION 2
Em & Am Chords

For online Audio Access to all of the audio tracks in this course, go to this address on the web:

http://cvls.com/extras/gm2/

E MINOR AND A MINOR CHORDS

Chords are three notes or more played together. Practice the Em and Am chords below and then work on switching from one chord to another. Strum down with your right hand.

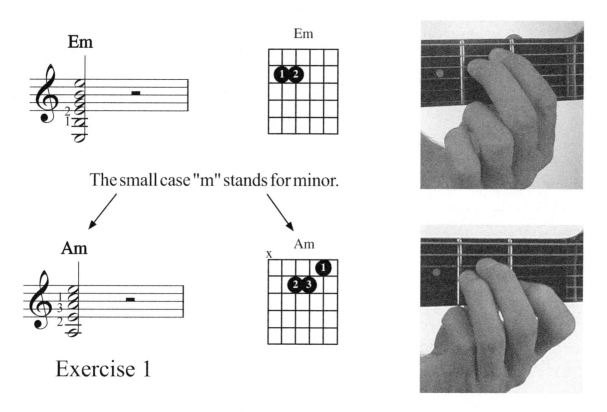

The small case "m" stands for minor.

Exercise 1

Practice playing the E minor chord. Try to make each note of the chord clear.

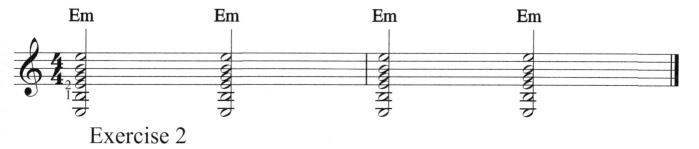

Exercise 2

Practice the A minor chord. Make each note clear.

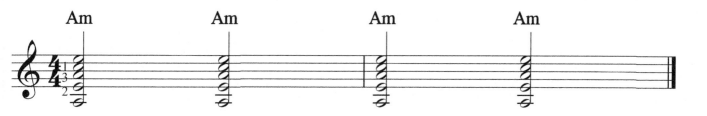

STRUMMING

Strum notation looks a little different than our regular notation. This notation should only be used when we already know the chords we are strumming. We will be using this strumming notation periodically throughout this course. The enlarged slash style head of a note means a strum. The note lasts its usual length.

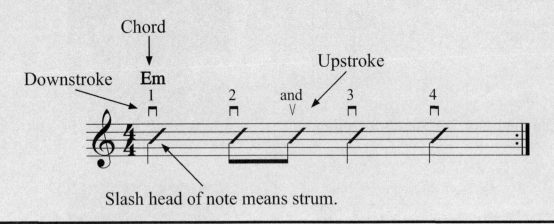

Slash head of note means strum.

Exercise 3

Practice the next three strum patterns using the E minor chord.

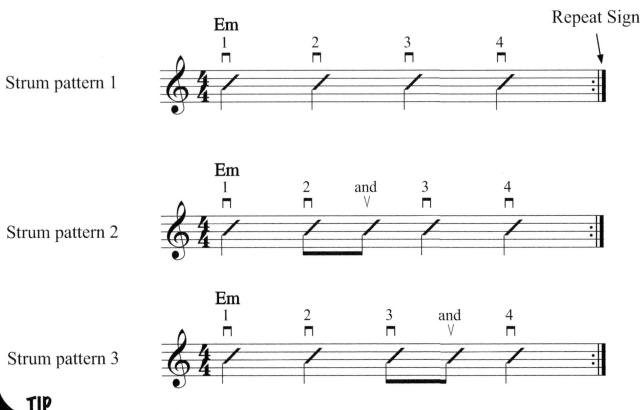

Strum pattern 1

Strum pattern 2

Strum pattern 3

TIP
Use a guitar humidifier in the winter to keep your guitar from drying out and cracking.

STRUM PATTERNS AND CHORD CHANGES

Practice strum patterns and chord changes in the next few exercises.

Exercise 4

When strumming E minor, strum from the 6th string down. When strumming A minor, strum from the 5th string down. In this exercise use strum pattern 1).

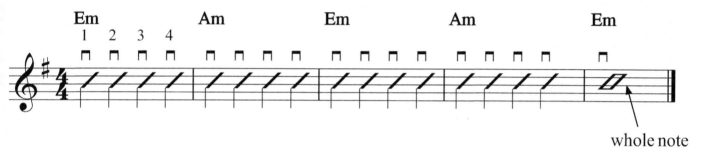

whole note

Exercise 5

In this exercise use strum pattern 2.

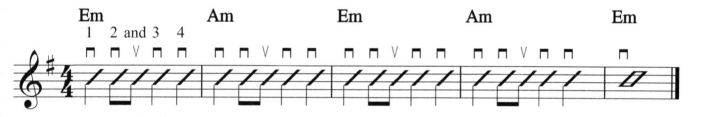

Exercise 6

Use strum pattern 3 in this exercise.

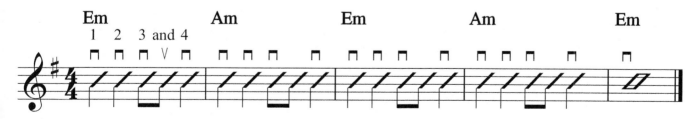

 Break your practice time into small chunks to increase retention.

17

MINOR STRUMMING INCIDENT

In this song, we are going to play the part of the rhythm guitarist. Play the chords and the strum patterns in time. When playing with the track, the band will play the melody. Practice slowly at first and then play along with the band.

STRUM AND MELODY

Now practice playing both chords and melody. In this tune, we use standard notation throughout. Eventually you will recognize chords by their combinations of notes.

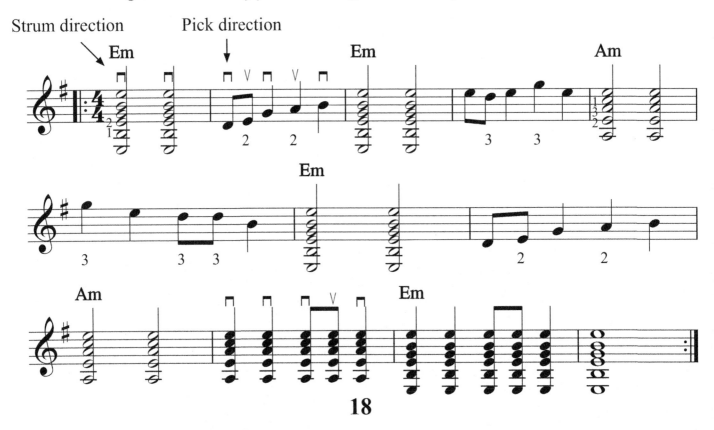

SIXTEENTH NOTES

We are going to start using sixteenth notes in our exercises and songs. Sixteenth notes are twice as fast as eighth notes. It is usually best to count sixteenth notes 1 ee and ah, 2 ee and ah, 3 ee and ah, 4 ee and ah. When sixteenth notes are connected together, they are often done so by using a beam. This makes it easier to read a series of sixteenth notes. We must also learn to recognize sixteenth notes rests.

SIXTEENTH NOTE   **SIXTEENTH NOTE REST**   **BEAMED SIXTEENTH NOTES**

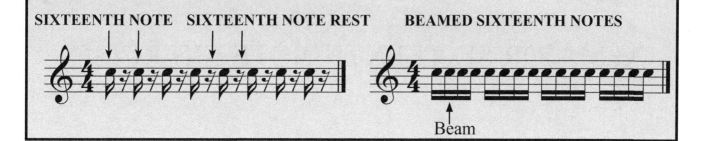

Beam

Exercise 7

Practice this exercise playing sixteenth notes. Be careful with the sixteenth note rests.

Exercise 8

Here is another exercise with sixteenth notes.

TIP *Practice in front of a mirror when working on technique. You will see much more from this angle.*

19

THE TWO OCTAVE G MAJOR SCALE

Practice the two octave G major scale in order to play the following G Major Sixteenth Note Exercise. Remember, when you see only 4 pick directions at the beginning of an exercise or song, it is to remind you to alternate your picking throughout.

Exercise 9

Practice this scale until you can play it smoothly.

3   2 3   2 4   2   1 3   2 3   3 2   3 1   2   4 2   3 2   3

G MAJOR SIXTEENTH NOTE EXERCISE

Exercise 10

This exercise utilizes both the two octave G major scale and sixteenth notes. Practice slowly at first and then gradually speed it up.

3 3 3 3   2 2 2 2 3 3 3 3   2 2 2 2 3 3 3 3

2 2 2 2 3 3 3 3   2 2 2 2   2 2 2 2 4 4 4 4

3 3 3 3 2 2 2 2   3 3 3 3   3 3 3 3 1 1 1 1

3 3 3 3 1 1 1 1   2 2 2 2   1 1 1 1   2 2 2 2

LET'S JAM! IN G MAJOR

This scaler melody is played over *G Ballad*, track 17 of the *Let's Jam! Unplugged* CD. The G major scale sounds great over this track and could be used for improvising or creating solos over a chord progression like this. Practice the sixteenth notes in this melody until you can play them smoothly and then play with the track.

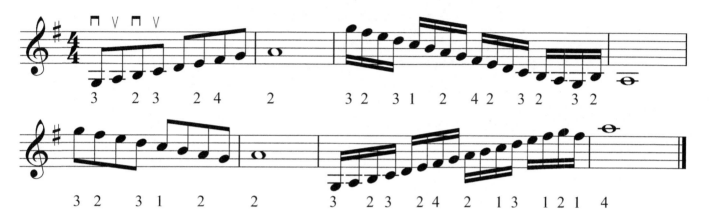

NINE POUND HAMMER

This song is a traditional bluegrass tune. The sixteenth note practice will come in handy because, when played up to speed, the eighth notes in bluegrass often feel like sixteenths. In other words - they are fast. Practice slow and smooth and then play with the band.

21

SECTION 3
G & D Chords & The A Major Scale

For online Audio Access to all of the audio tracks in this course, go to this address on the web:

http://cvls.com/extras/gm2/

G MAJOR AND D7 CHORDS

Add G major and D7 to our known chords. First practice making each chord.

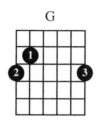
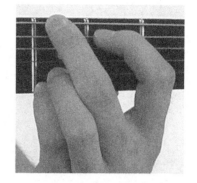

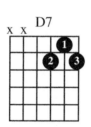

Exercise 11

Practice playing the G major chord.

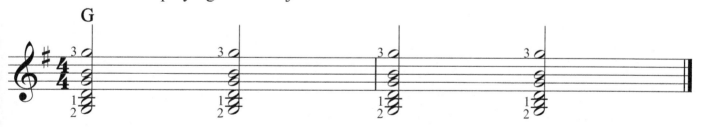

Exercise 12

Practice playing the D7 chord.

A CHORD PROGRESSION IN G MAJOR

Practice the strum patterns and chord changes in the next few exercises.

Exercise 13

In this exercise we will work on a new chord progression. Practice changing from one chord to the next.

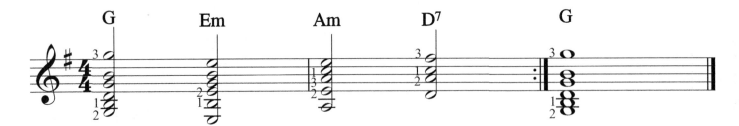

Exercise 14

This exercise demonstrates one of the most common strum patterns used on guitar.

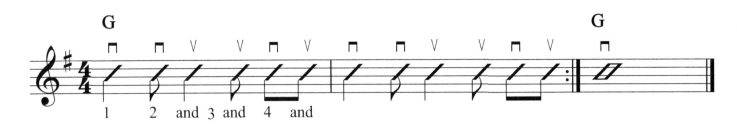

G MAJOR SONG

Now put this all together and play rhythm to *G Major Song*. Play the Repeat 8 times.

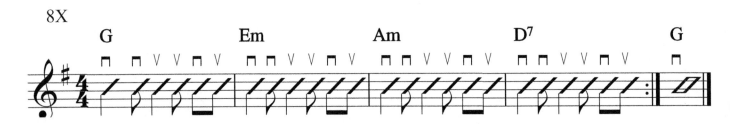

 *Guitars should be set up by a luthier if you change gauges of strings.*

THE A MAJOR SCALE

Practice the two octave A major scale below.

Exercise 15

Practice the A major scale until you can play it smoothly. Take special note of the key signature. There are three sharps: F sharp, C sharp, and G sharp. Make sure you sharp these three notes throughout this exercise. Remember a sharp raises a note one fret.

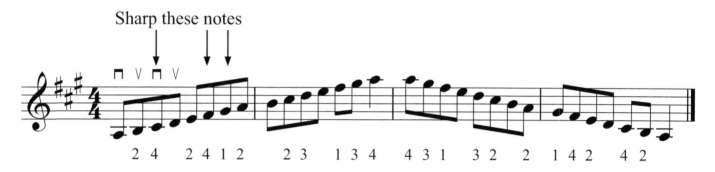

SIXTEENTH AND EIGHTH NOTE COMBO

Exercise 16

First practice reading the sixteenth note rhythmic figure in Exercise 16 and then practice playing Exercise 17 which has more complex combinations.

Exercise 17

MIXING RHYTHMS EXERCISE

Exercise 18

This exercise mixes many rhythms together. This will help solidify our sense of time and subdivisions of the beat.

ANGELS WE HAVE HEARD ON HIGH

This is a traditional Christmas song with a sixteenth note variation to finish.

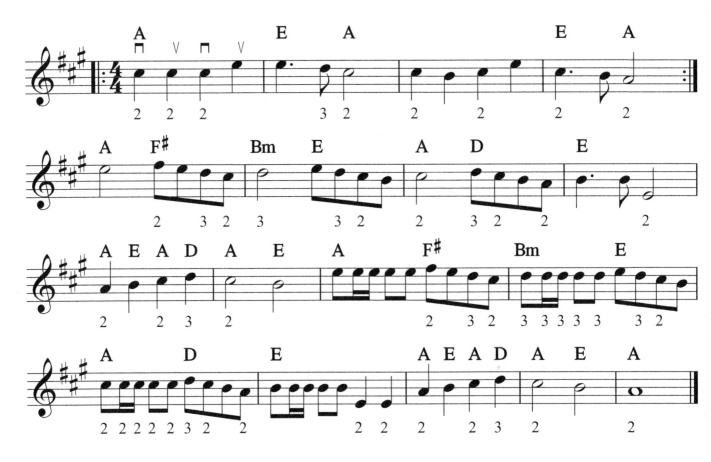

LET'S JAM! IN A MAJOR

This tune is a melody played over *A Major Groove*, track 2 of the *Let's Jam! Unplugged* CD. You can improvise using the A major scale or just practice the scale over the track. In this case, we are playing a specific melody using the A major scale. Practice until you can play it smoothly and then try it with the track.

PLAYING THIRDS IN A

Exercise 19

This exercise is a harmony exercise in the key of A. Practice it slow and smoothly and be careful with the fingerings. Notice only downstrokes are used.

TIP *Electronic tuners are the best way to tune a guitar.*

27

SECTION 4
E7, A7, & B7 Chords and The E Blues Scale

For online Audio Access to all of the audio tracks in this course, go to this address on the web:

http://cvls.com/extras/gm2/

E7, A7, AND B7 CHORDS

Practice the E7, A7, and B7 chords below.

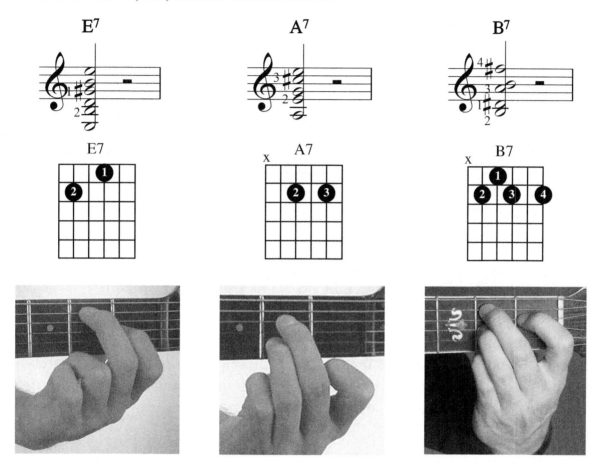

Exercise 20

Practice playing E7, A7, and B7 in the exercise below.

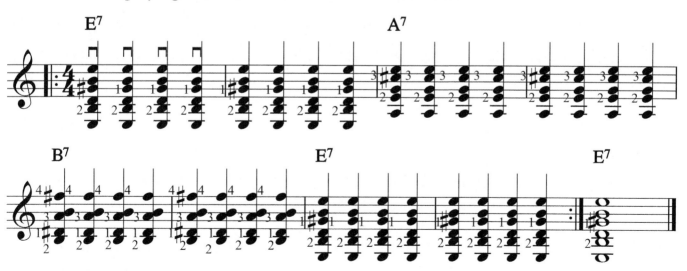

Exercise 21

Practice the strum pattern in this exercise. We are going to use it in the next song where we play rhythm guitar with the band.

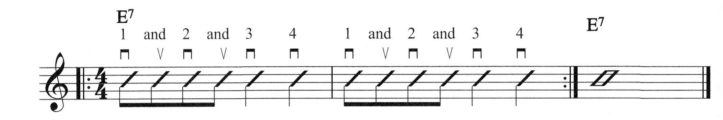

12 BAR BLUES IN E RHYTHM

In this tune we once again adopt the role of the rhythm guitar player. The 12 bar blues chord progression is one of the most commonly used chord progressions in music. Learn it well as you will definitely use it in the future. Play the chords and the strum pattern in time with the band.

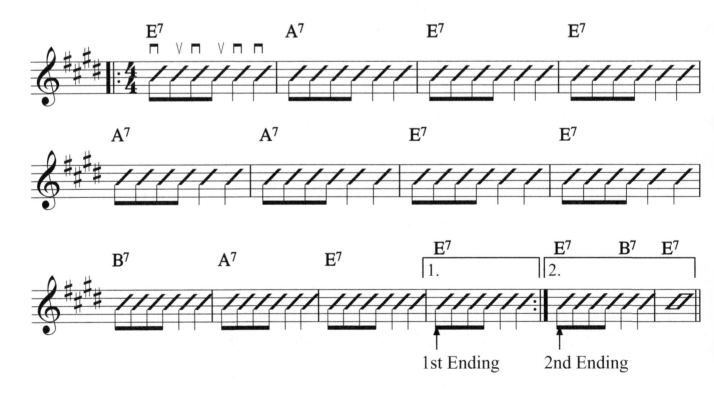

THE E BLUES SCALE

The E blues scale is a widely used scale on guitar. Practice the scale below as it will prove very useful.

Exercise 22

Practice the E blues scale. This exercise takes us through two octaves forwards and backwards

E MINOR BLUES

This tune utilizes the E blues scale against a minor chord progression. Play with the band or play it as a solo piece.

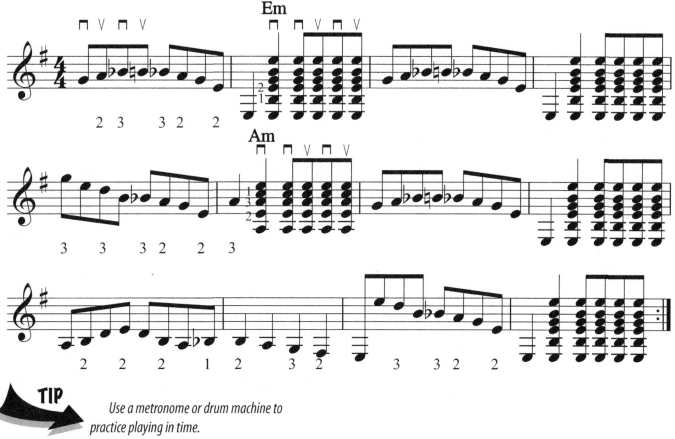

TIP *Use a metronome or drum machine to practice playing in time.*

31

TRIPLETS

Triplet eighth notes play three times per beat (quarter note). It is generally a good idea to accent the first beat of every triplet. To count triplets count tri-pa-let or 1 and ah.

Remember 1 quarter note, 2 eighth notes, and a triplet take up the same amount of time.

Exercise 23

Practice the triplets in this exercise. Try accenting the first note of each triplet.

Exercise 24

This is another exercise playing triplets but in E Major. (Key of E page 57 *Guitar Method Book 1*). Be careful of the sharps (F sharp, C sharp, G sharp, D sharp).

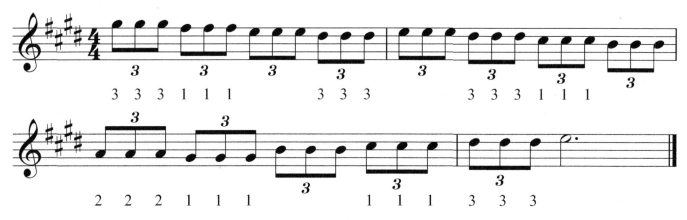

JESU, JOY OF MAN'S DESIRING

This song is a classic Bach melody. It is full of triplets.

J.S. Bach

THREE TIMES THE CURE

In *Three Times The Cure* we work on mixing up rhythms. You must be able to switch from quarter notes to eighth notes to triplets. When reading this tune notice the bass notes are ringing underneath the melody notes. For example in bar two the note G is ringing while you are playing the notes above it. Listen to the audio example and count along with it. This will make it clear to you.

TIP *Memorize the notes on the guitar as you find them in this book. This will help you learn quicker.*

E MINOR PENTATONIC SEQUENCES AND LET'S JAM!

The next two exercises are sequences, or repeated patterns, of the E minor pentatonic scale. Practice each until you can play it smoothly and then try playing each sequence with the track *Steady in Em* from the *Let's Jam! Unplugged CD*.

Exercise 25

This first sequence is all eighth notes. Play two strings of the E minor pentatonic scale (page 38 of *Guitar Method Book 1*) and then go back one. (Understanding the pentatonic scale page 33 of *The Guitarist's Music Theory Book*). Once you get to the top, go backwards.

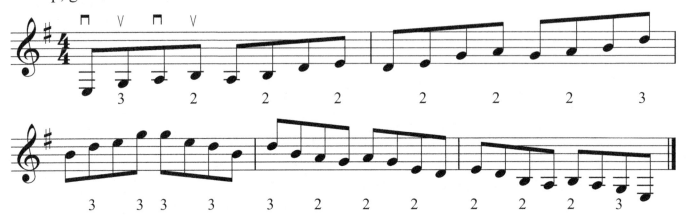

Exercise 26

This sequence is playing triplets. Play three strings of the E minor pentatonic scale and then go back two. Once you get to the highest note, go backwards.

TIP → *The **Let's Jam! CDs** are great for practicing scales and licks.*

34

SECTION 5
A, D, & E Chords and Playing In
Higher Positions

For online Audio Access to all of the audio tracks in this course, go to this address on the web:

http://cvls.com/extras/gm2/

A, D, AND E CHORDS

Practice the A, D and E chords below.

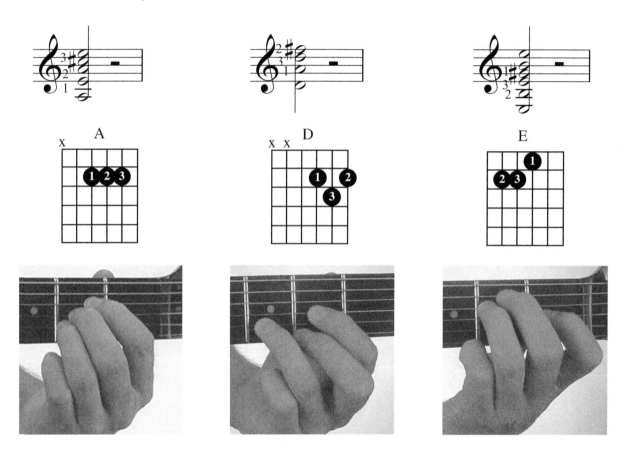

Exercise 27

Practice playing A, D, and E chords in the exercise below.

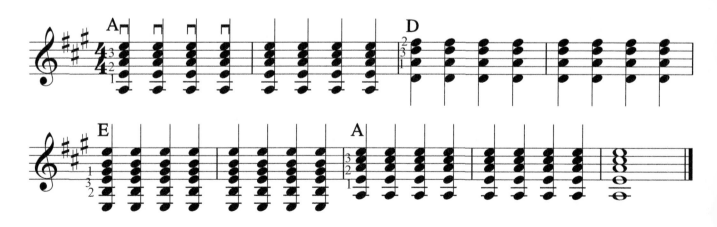

A good strap should be connected to the guitar by a set of strap locks.

Exercise 28

Practice the strum pattern in this exercise. We are going to use it in the next song.

AMAZING GRACE

Play rhythm guitar while the band plays the melody. The top staff is the melody and the bottom staff is the rhythm guitar part.

TIP

Keep your strumming strokes small and the same length for more control.

ANOTHER G MAJOR CHORD

In order to play the following exercises and songs, we must learn another way to play G major. This is termed *another voicing of the chord*. It is very similar to our previous version of G major and can be used interchangeably with it. Practice the G major chord below.

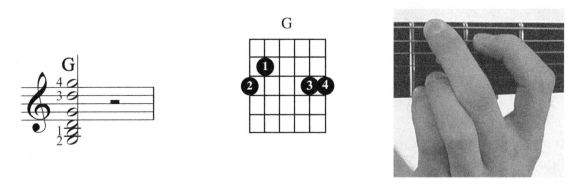

Exercise 29

Practice the G major chord in this exercise.

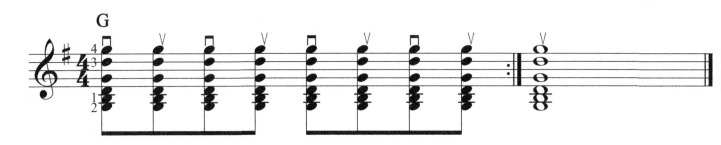

Exercise 30

Practice this strum pattern with the G major chord. It will be used in our next song.

TIP *Never use furniture polish on your guitar. Use guitar polish and a guitar cloth.*

THE BOTTOM LINE

In this song we are going to play chords and a bass line. Be careful with the fingering and make sure the bass line is treated like a melody.

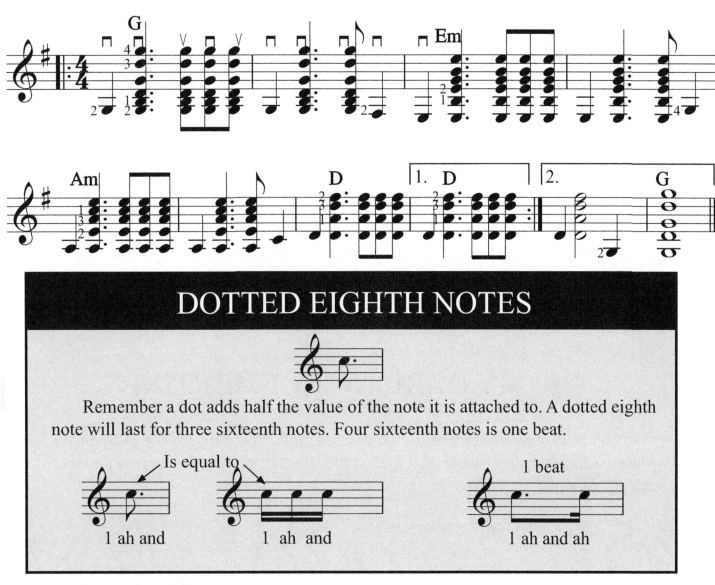

DOTTED EIGHTH NOTES

Remember a dot adds half the value of the note it is attached to. A dotted eighth note will last for three sixteenth notes. Four sixteenth notes is one beat.

Exercise 31

Practice the exercise below and pay special attention to the dotted eighth notes.

O CHRISTMAS TREE

One of my all time favorite Christmas melodies. This arrangement highlights the use of dotted eighth notes. Be careful with the rhythms. When you can play it smoothly, try it with the band.

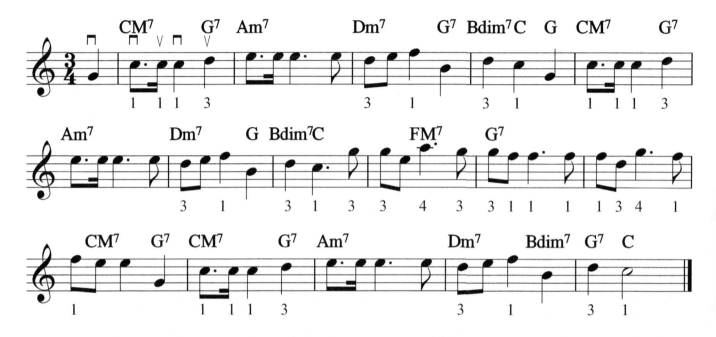

OH, MY DARLING CLEMENTINE

This is another song that uses the dotted eighth note. This tune is played solo since it combines chords and melody. Let the chord tones ring as much as possible during this song.

TIP

When playing a solo piece be sure to include dynamics or playing louder and softer in a musical manner.

PLAYING IN HIGHER POSITIONS

When moving up the neck out of first position, these icons are used. The number tells the player what string to play that particular note on. We have been playing the note E as the open first string. It could, however, be played on the 2nd string 5th fret, the 3rd string 9th fret, or the 4th string 14th fret.

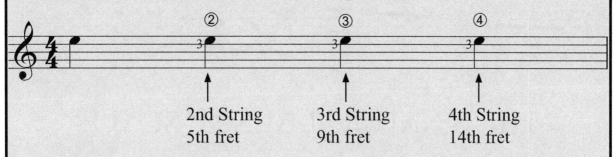

Sometimes the fingering is enough to tell you where it is played and there will not be a circled number. It depends entirely upon the circumstance. Here are a few common examples. The 5th fret 2nd string is the same note as the open 1st string (E). The 4th fret 3rd string is the same note as the open 2nd string (B). The 5th fret 4th string is the same note as the open 3rd string (G). The 5th fret 5th string is the same note as the open 4th string (D). The 5th fret 6th string is the same note as the open 5th string (A). In all these cases, the fingering should be enough to tell you when it isn't an open string.

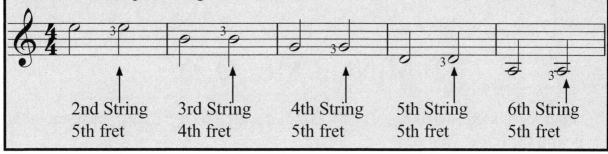

Exercise 32

Practice playing the notes where indicated. Pay close attention to string indicators and fingering.

41

SCALES USING HIGHER POSITION NOTES

Exercise 33

We have played the G major scale before. Now practice the G Major scale in a higher position using no open strings. Pay very careful attention to the fingering and the string indicators.

THE B NATURAL MINOR SCALE

Exercise 34

The scale below is the B natural minor scale. Again, pay very close attention to the fingering and the string indicators. Also notice that we have added a new note. The last note of this exercise is the note B at the 7th fret, 1st string.

1st String
7th fret

B MINOR MELODY

Practice this tune that is based on the B minor scale. Once you can play it smoothly, try it with the track.

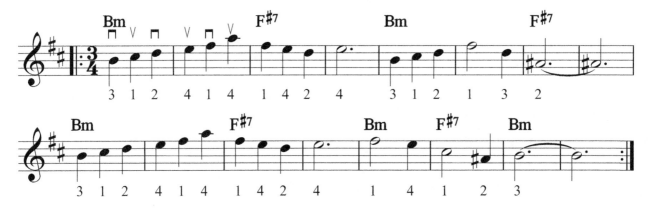

SECTION 6
C, Dm, & G7 Chords and 6/8 Time

For online Audio Access to all of the audio tracks in this course, go to this address on the web:

http://cvls.com/extras/gm2/

C, D MINOR, AND G7 CHORDS

Practice the C, D minor and G7 chords below.

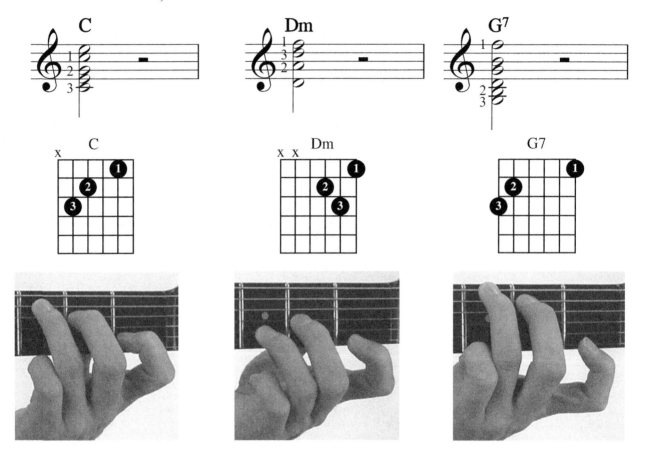

Exercise 35

Practice playing C, D minor, and G7 chords in the exercises below.

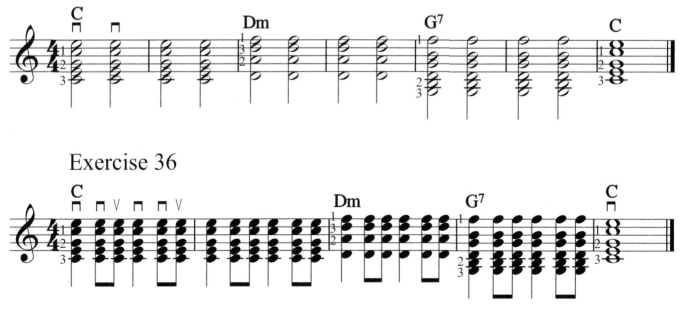

Exercise 36

JUST IN TIME

This song uses the chords we have learned and the strum pattern we have just worked on with a small variation occurring every other measure. In this tune you are the rhythm guitar player, so keep time playing with the track. Play the repeat 4 times.

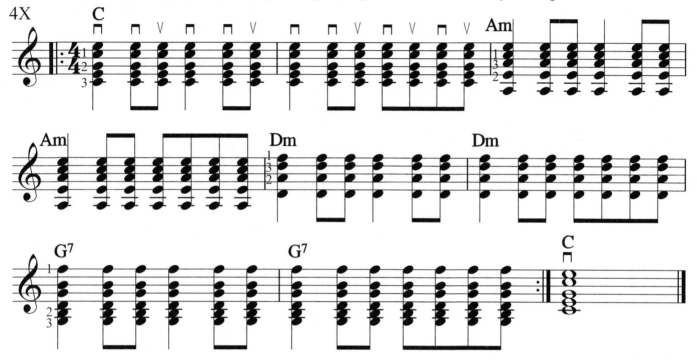

ARPEGGIOS IN C

This tune uses arpeggios, which means playing one note of a chord at a time. Let the notes ring together as much as possible. Make the chord shapes and stay with them until you must change.

TIP

There are only 12 notes to play but there are an infinite amount of rhythms and dynamics.

45

Exercise 37

This is another arpeggio exercise. Practice this exercise until it sounds smooth and connected.

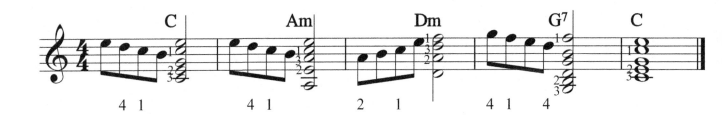

BASS LINE WALTZ

In *Bass Line Waltz,* we will play chords and an alternating bass line. There is no accompaniment for this tune, so play the bass notes big and be musical.

SIX EIGHT TIME

Six Eight time falls into the category of "complex time". This means each beat is divided by three instead of two. There are two beats in each measure and each beat consists of three eighth notes. **The beat in six eight time is a dotted quarter note.** Remember, in "simple time" like four four or three four time, each beat is divided by two. An easy way to think of **six eight** time is each measure has **six eighth** notes.

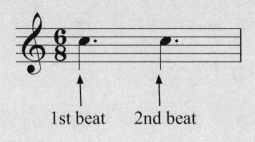

1st beat   2nd beat

1   and   ah   2   and   ah

Each beat divided into three eight notes.

Exercise 38

Practice this melody in 6/8 time. Remember each beat is divided by three and the dotted quarter note is one beat.

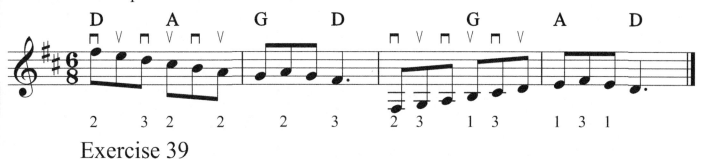

Exercise 39

Here is another melody in 6/8 time. This time be careful with the quarter notes. Remember each beat is divided into three eighth notes and a quarter note only lasts for two of those eighth notes.

47

CANARIOS MELODY

Canarios is a famous melody in 6/8 time. This is a shortened version of the piece that is commonly played on the classical guitar.

ARPEGGIOS IN 6/8

Here is a wide skipping arpeggio in 6/8 time. Pay attention to the pick directions at the beginning as they give you an indicator on how to approach this exercise.

WE THREE KINGS

We Three Kings is in 6/8 time. This is a harmonized melody that briefly moves out of first position.

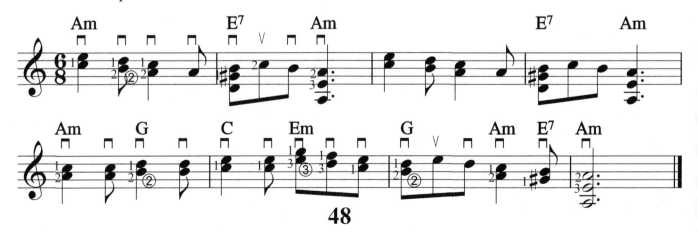

SECTION 7

DM7, FM7 Chords, The Gm Pentatonic Scale, and 9/8 & 12/8 Time

For online Audio Access to all of the audio tracks in this course, go to this address on the web:

http://cvls.com/extras/gm2/

CM7 AND FM7 CHORDS

Practice the CM7(C major 7th) and FM7(F major seventh) chords below. Major seventh chords sound more complex to the ear and are generally pretty sounding chords.

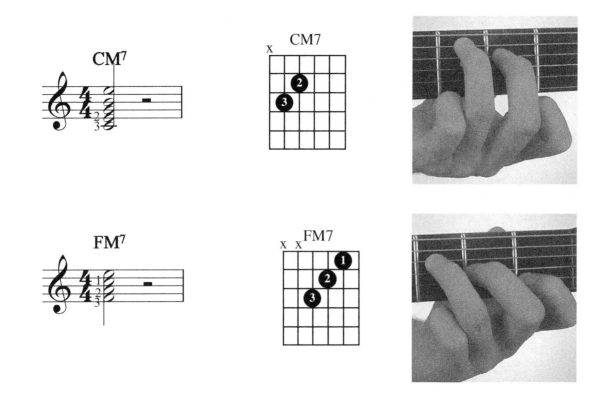

Exercise 40

Practice playing the CM7 and FM7 chords below. Practice smooth chord changes.

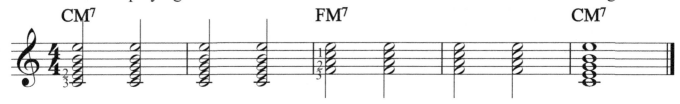

Exercise 41

Now practice a strum pattern with the same chords.

SMOOTH MOVE

This song uses the chords we have learned and the strum pattern we have just worked on with a small variation occurring every other measure. In this tune, you are the rhythm guitar player so practice keeping time playing with the track. Play the repeat 4 times.

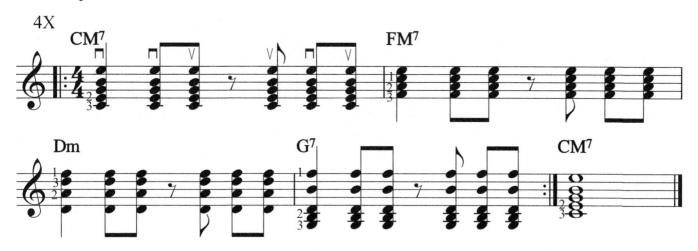

COLOR MY CHORDS

Using the same chords we have just learned, practice the arpeggios in the exercise below. Let the notes ring together as much as possible.

 *When playing guitar, use the lightest touch possible with your left hand that will get a clear note.*

51

B FLAT AT THE 6TH FRET

The note B flat below the staff can be played in two places. The 1st fret 5th string or the 6th fret 6th string.

The note B flat above the staff can be bound at the sixth fret first string.

THE G MINOR PENTATONIC SCALE

The pentatonic scales are widely used for soloing on the guitar. Practice the next few exercises using the G minor pentatonic scale.

Exercise 42

Play the G minor pentatonic scale. Follow the fingerings and be aware of the note B flat on the sixth and first strings.

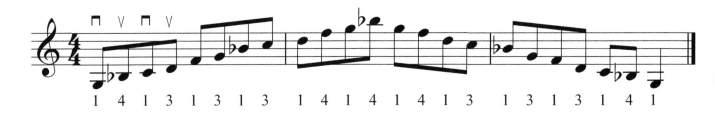

1 4 1 3 1 3 1 3   1 4 1 4 1 4 1 3   1 3 1 3 1 4 1

A good teacher can dramatically increase your rate of learning.

B FLAT AND G MINOR KEY SIGNATURE

The correct key signature for both G minor and B flat major consists of two accidentals: B flat and E flat.

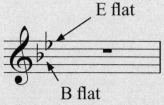

B flat major and G minor have the same key signature. They are said to be **relative major and minor.**

Exercise 43

This exercise is a sequence. Practice this sequence using the G minor pentatonic scale.

4 1 4 1 4 1 3 1   3 1 3 1 3 1 3 1   3 1 4 1

Exercise 44

This exercise is the same sequence as the previous exercise but this time in reverse. Practice this sequence.

1 4 1 3 1 3 1 3   1 3 1 3 1 3 1 4   1 4 1 4

TIP

Have your guitar set up twice a year. Once in the spring and once in the fall.

G MINOR JAM

The next couple of exercises are sequences using the G minor pentatonic scale. Practice them until you can play them smoothly and then play along with the track *Gm Blues* from the *Let's Jam! More Blues and Rock* CD.

Exercise 45

This first sequence is all eighth notes. Play three strings of the G minor pentatonic scale and then go back two. Once you get to the highest note, play the sequence backwards.

Exercise 46

This is the same sequence but this time playing triplets. Play three strings of the G minor pentatonic scale and then go back two. Once you get to the highest note play the sequence backwards.

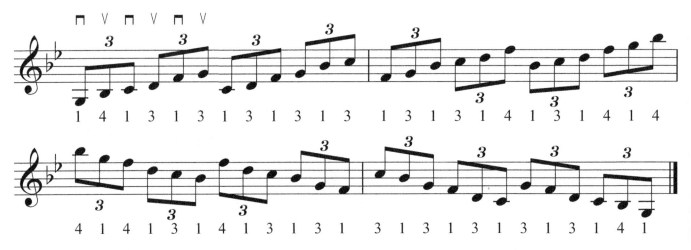

 TIP

When soloing, the goal is to create a melody. Hopefully create an interesting one.

54

NINE EIGHT AND TWELVE EIGHT TIME

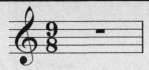 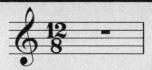

Nine eight time and twelve eight time are very much like six eight time. All are complex time since the beat is divided by three eighth notes and the dotted quarter note is the beat. Nine eight time has three beats per measure and twelve eight time has four beats per measure. Remember **nine eight time has nine eighth notes** and **twelve eight time has twelve eighth notes** per measure.

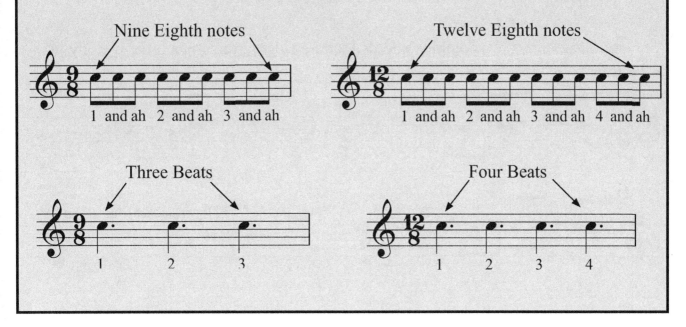

Exercise 47

Practice this melody in 9/8 time. Remember each beat is divided by three and the dotted quarter note equals one beat.

 **TIP**

*For more scales try **The Guitarist's Scale Book** by Watch & Learn.*

Exercise 48

Here is an exercise in 12/8 time. This exercise is in the key of A. Be careful with the sharps.

Exercise 49

In this exercise we combine chords that are ringing underneath the melody in 9/8 time.

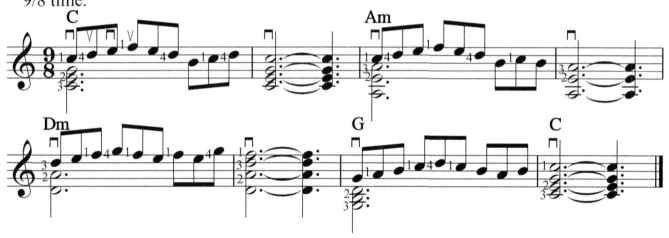

Exercise 50

Next we will play a C major scale exercise in 12/8 time. Be careful with the fingerings and notice there are no open strings used. This is a powerful drill to develop scale proficiency.

Exercise 51

This exercise in 12/8 time has a very common rhythm found in the blues. Practice this exercise until it feels natural in order to go on to the next blues song. Remember, the beats are divided into three eighth notes, and be careful with the quarter note eighth note combination.

FEELING THEM BLUES

This song is a twelve bar blues and uses the rhythmic figure learned in the previous exercise. Practice it slowly at first and then play with the track.

TIP *Practice slow and relaxed.*

THE WATER IS WIDE

This tune is meant to be played solo. As your note reading progresses you will run across chords or combinations of notes that you haven't played before. This means you will have to depend on your note reading skills to figure them out. B minor seven may be an example of this in our next song.

MY COUNTRY 'TIS OF THEE

In this song, the chord names are left out as it becomes more important to recognize chords simply from the notation.

Printed in Great Britain
by Amazon